Our Neighbor, the Moon!

This course was written by
Naturally Curious Expert
Deborah McArthur

*Deborah is a science educator who loves connecting others
to the wonders of the physical and natural world.*

Printed by CreateSpace

ISBN 978-1-942403-11-1

www.benaturallycurious.com

Many activities in this book make use of printed materials. If you prefer not to cut them directly from this book, please visit the URL listed below and enter the code for a supplemental PDF containing all printable materials.

URL: www.benaturallycurious.com/moon-printables/

password: **wane**

Table of Contents

Required materials: light-colored ball, black marker, flashlight, paper, eight Oreo sandwich cookies, butter knife, colored pens, chalk, concrete for drawing (driveway, sidewalk, or playground), scissors, bingo card markers (e.g., pennies, pebbles, or poker chips), hat or pouch

A Tour of the Moon with Selene

Hi! I'm Selene, and I live on the moon. The moon is an amazing place. I'd love to show you around and tell you about my LUNAR home. The moon and Earth have a lot of things in common, and a lot of things are also quite different.

Have you looked closely at the moon and noticed any details and patterns? Come on a tour with me. You can be a selenologist!

A **selenologist** is a person who studies selenology, the branch of astronomy that deals with the moon. *Selene* is the Greek word for "moon."

Let's start with the basics. The moon's orbit is slightly oval. The moon is closer to the Earth at some times than at other times. On average, the moon is about 239,000 miles, or 387,000 kilometers, away from Earth. Those are big numbers! Try to imagine traveling around Earth's equator 10 times. That would be similar to the distance you'd have to travel to get to the moon.

How big do you think the moon is compared to Earth? Since it's so far away, it looks small in the sky, but its diameter is actually one-fourth the size of Earth's. That's about the size of the continents of North or South America.

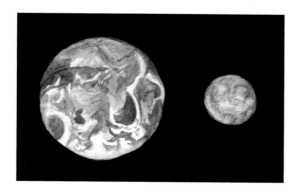

Lunar means having to do with the moon.

It would take around fifty moons to fill up as much space as one Earth.

When you look at the moon, what do you notice about its surface? Have you observed the light and dark parts of the moon? Some people see shapes in these light and dark features. A man. A bunny. Or Swiss cheese. What do you see?

Let's go on a moon walk! Or, should we say, a moon bounce? The moon has much less GRAVITY than Earth because it has less mass. Gravity keeps you on the ground on Earth—but on the moon, the pull is much less.

Look down! A big difference between Earth and the moon is right at your feet. A fine powder of rock and volcanic glass called *regolith* covers the moon's surface. No dirt. No soil. So nothing living can grow on the moon.

What about liquid water? Does the moon have any oceans or seas?

> There is no soil on the moon—just a powdery rock called *regolith*.

If you said no, you are right. It's interesting that early selenologists thought the dark patches on the moon were oceans similar to those on Earth. To this day, the dark areas of the moon have watery names. These areas of heavy volcanic rock are called MARIA (one is called a MARE). They have cool names, too. The largest is called the Ocean of Storms. There is the Sea of Tranquility, and the *mare nubium*, which is the Sea of Clouds.

> The dark parts of the moon are called *maria*.

Mare comes from the Latin word *mar*, which means "sea."

Most of the moon's surface—85%—is light-colored, rocky highlands called TERRAE, marked by round CRATERS (which make the moon look like Swiss cheese). These craters are named for famous astronomers and thinkers, include Craters Copernicus, Keplar, Tycho, and Plato.

> The light parts of the moon are called *terrae*.

Hold on! Do you feel the moon moving? Similar to Earth, the moon ROTATES, or spins on its axis. Stand up and turn around once in place. You just rotated!

The moon also REVOLVES, or ORBITS, around Earth. To understand this motion, place an object on the floor. Now walk around it in a circle while keeping the same distance from it. You just revolved around it!

Now, orbit the object again with the front of your body facing the object in the middle the whole time. You are rotating as you revolve.

This is what the moon does when it's moving around Earth, so the same side of the moon is always facing Earth. You Earthlings call the half of the moon that faces Earth the NEAR side. Can you guess what the other side of the moon is called? The FAR side!

The same side of the moon always faces Earth.

Earth rotates once every day (24 hours) and revolves around the sun once every year (365 days). The time the moon takes to rotate and revolve around Earth is the same.

Do you have a favorite PHASE, or shape, of the moon? Do you like it when the full moon is shining bright or when the moon looks like a bowl full of milk? You have probably observed that the moon looks different and changes shape over time. But how does this happen?

The phases of the moon have to do with the ORBIT and your LINE OF SIGHT—in other words, where the moon is in its orbit around Earth and how you see it from Earth. Only certain parts of the near side of the moon are visible from Earth during different parts of the lunar month. The combination of sunlit and dark parts of the moon creates the phases. Let's break it down phase by phase.

Start with the NEW moon. This is when you can't really see the moon from Earth. The moon is in between the sun and Earth in its orbit. The sun is shining on the FAR side of the moon, so you Earthlings have dark nights.

> The moon reflects light from the sun.

> The *phase* of the moon you see depends on where it is in the lunar *orbit* and your *line of sight.*

NEW moon: When the moon is between the sun and Earth

This is how the new moon looks to you on Earth.

Now let's check out the FULL moon phase—when the near side is completely lit up. A full moon happens when the moon and sun are on the opposite sides of Earth.

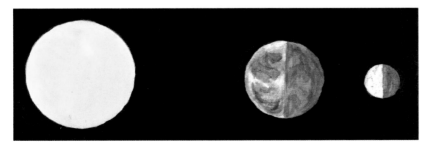

FULL moon: When the moon and sun are on the opposite sides of Earth.

This how the full moon looks to you on Earth.

Next, let's look at the moon when it's at a 90-degree angle from the sun. From your line of sight on Earth, you only see half of the moon's near side lit up. This is called the HALF moon phase. The half moon in the picture below is also called a first quarter moon because the moon is one-quarter of the way around its orbit.

HALF moon: When the moon is at a 90-degree angle from the sun.

Now, there's a fun but tricky point we have to add. How some of the moon phases look to you depends on where on the Earth you are! In the Northern Hemisphere, the light part of the moon might be on one side, but in the southern hemisphere that light part will be flipped from right to left (or vice versa). It's just like looking at an object in front of you—if the object doesn't move, but YOU flip upside down, the object will appear flipped from right to left. So, go ahead and figure out which hemisphere you are in, and make sure to follow along with those pictures!

NORTHERN HEMISPHERE

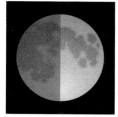

This is how the First Quarter (Half) moon looks to you on Earth in the Northern Hemisphere.

SOUTHERN HEMISPHERE

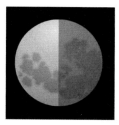

This is how the First Quarter (Half) moon looks to you on Earth in the Southern Hemisphere.

New moon. Full moon. Half moon. What other moon phases are there? How about the thin sliver of moon that looks like the tip of your fingernail? This is the CRESCENT phase, which comes between the new moon and half moon phases.

Can you find the different crescent moons in the moon cycle below?

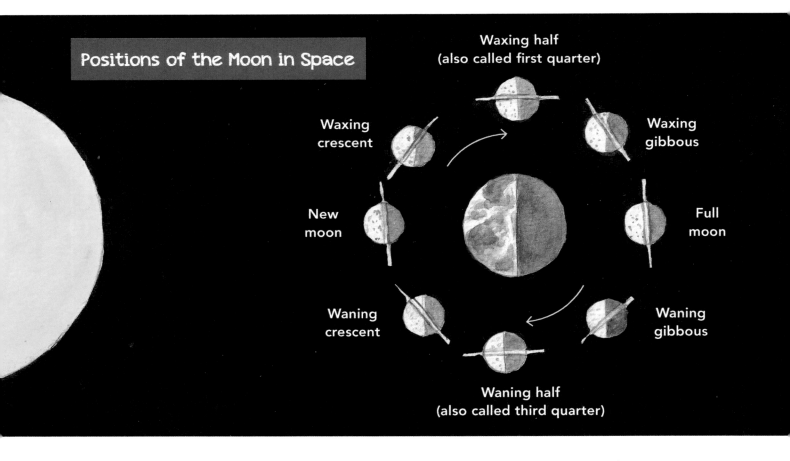

Positions of the Moon in Space

Waxing half
(also called first quarter)

Waxing crescent

Waxing gibbous

New moon

Full moon

Waning crescent

Waning gibbous

Waning half
(also called third quarter)

This is how the crescent moons would look to you on Earth:

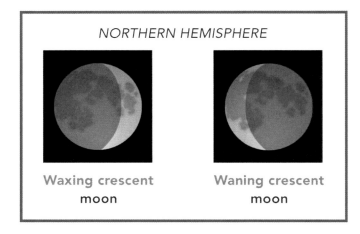

NORTHERN HEMISPHERE

Waxing crescent moon

Waning crescent moon

SOUTHERN HEMISPHERE

Waxing crescent moon

Waning crescent moon

Another moon phase is between the half moon and the full moon. This is called the GIBBOUS moon.

Can you find the different gibbous moons in the moon cycle on page 10? This is how the gibbous moons would look to you on Earth:

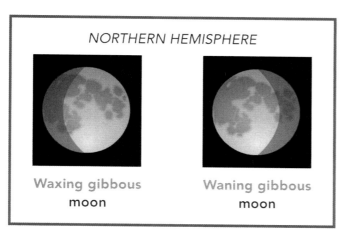

NORTHERN HEMISPHERE

Waxing gibbous
moon

Waning gibbous
moon

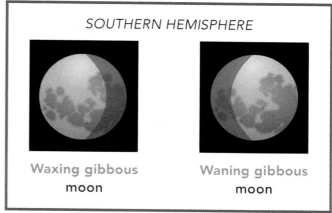

SOUTHERN HEMISPHERE

Waxing gibbous
moon

Waning gibbous
moon

The word **gibbous** comes from the Latin word *gibbus*, which means "hump."

You're on your way to being a great selenologist! There are a couple of other important words you need to know, and then you're ready to talk all about the moon phases:

WAXING is the word for getting bigger each day. WANING means getting smaller.

If you are in the Northern Hemisphere, a very helpful phrase is "Moon on the right, getting bigger every night." What that means is if the light part of the moon is on the right, then it is WAXING (and if it is on the left, it would be WANING).

In the Southern Hemisphere the opposite is true. If the light part of the moon is on the left, then it is WAXING (and if it is on the right, it is WANING).

Now you can combine the phases of the moon (crescent, gibbous, half) with whether it is getting bigger or smaller (waxing or waning) so you can describe the entire lunar CYCLE!

A **cycle** is something that repeats itself.

A *waxing* moon is getting bigger, toward a *full* moon.

A *waning* moon is getting smaller, toward a *new* moon.

That concludes our tour of the moon. Isn't it fascinating? And it is *so* important to get to know your neighbors. I'll be seeing you around. Remember to keep your eye on the sky and say hi as the moon goes by!

NORTHERN HEMISPHERE

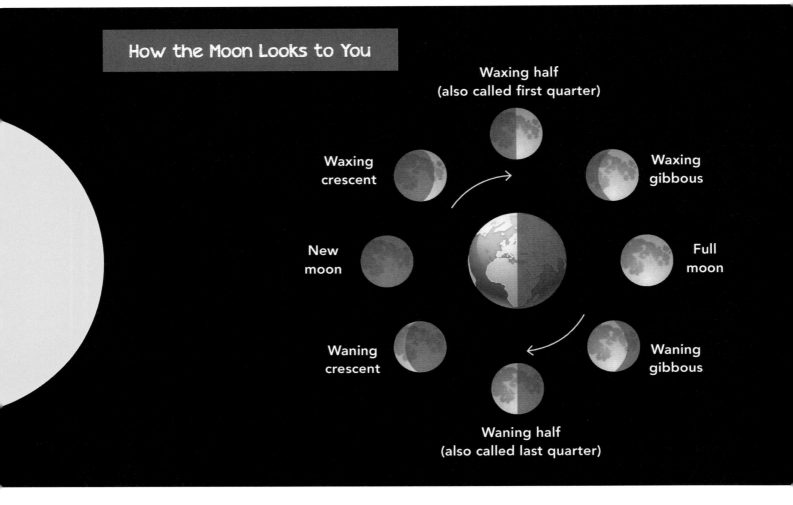

How the Moon Looks to You

Waxing half
(also called first quarter)

Waxing crescent

Waxing gibbous

New moon

Full moon

Waning crescent

Waning gibbous

Waning half
(also called last quarter)

SOUTHERN HEMISPHERE

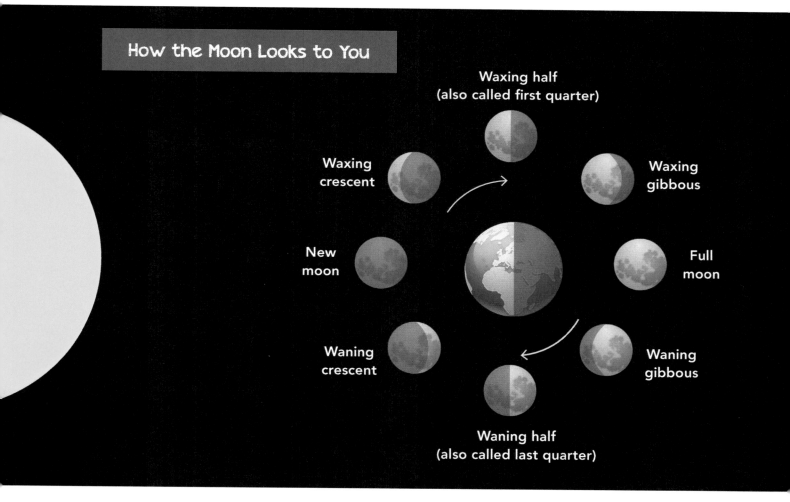

How the Moon Looks to You

Waxing half
(also called first quarter)

Waxing
crescent

Waxing
gibbous

New
moon

Full
moon

Waning
crescent

Waning
gibbous

Waning half
(also called last quarter)

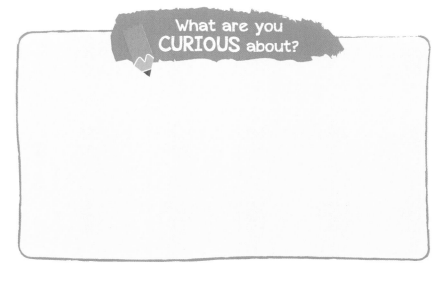

What are you
CURIOUS about?

Orbit Around Earth!

INSTRUCTIONS

Now that you know the names for the phases of the moon and the terms *waxing* and *waning*, let's model the movement of the moon's orbit to better understand how seeing phases of the moon is all about your line of sight from Earth. Remember, the moon does not have any light of its own—it only reflects the light of the sun. And the shape you see depends on how much of the lit-up moon is in your line of sight.

Preparation

Color half of the ball with a black marker. The blackened side always faces away from the sun (which is simulated by the flashlight).

> **MATERIALS**
> - light-colored ball
> - black marker
> - flashlight
> - dark room
> - 2–3 people

1. **Choose one person to be the sun.** This person holds the flashlight, pointing it toward Earth when the lights are turned out. (With only two people, set the flashlight on a table.)

2. **Choose someone to be the moon.** This person will walk in a circle "orbiting" around Earth. It is very important for this person to hold the light side of the ball (the side that hasn't been colored with the marker), which always faces the sun.

3. **Choose who will start as Earth.** This person stands 8–10 feet in front of the sun, allowing room for the moon to orbit.

Challenge

- The person who is Earth will report how much of the moon, or which phase of the moon, he or she sees as the moon orbits. This person can use the moon phase chart from the end of the story as a reference.

- Start with the moon directly in between Earth and the sun. Do you see any of the lit-up side of the moon from Earth? What phase of the moon do we call this? (new moon)

- **In the Northern Hemisphere**: Have the moon walk in a **counterclockwise** circle (orbit) to the opposite side of Earth from the sun. Now do you see any of the lit-up side of the moon? If so, how much? What phase of the moon do we call this? (full moon)

  In the Southern Hemisphere: Have the moon walk in a **clockwise** circle (orbit) to the opposite side of Earth from the sun. Now do you see any of the lit-up side of the moon? If so, how much? What phase of the moon do we call this? (full moon)

Orbit Around Earth!

INSTRUCTIONS (continued)

- Next, have the moon move to 90 degrees from the sun. (Make sure the light side of the moon is facing the sun!) Do you see any of the lit-up side of the moon from Earth? If so, how much? What phase of the moon do we call this? (half moon)

- The moon should continue to orbit so Earth observes the crescent and gibbous phases.

- Orbiting counterclockwise (Northern Hemisphere) or clockwise (Southern Hemisphere) around Earth, identify the whole moon cycle from new moon to waxing crescent to waxing half to waxing gibbous to full moon and back to new moon.

Switch roles so different people represent Earth, the moon, and the sun. Repeat the orbiting. Switch again so everyone has a chance to be Earth, the moon, and the sun.

Cookie Phases

INSTRUCTIONS

Let's make a diagram of the lunar cycle using cookies to show the phases of the moon.

Preparation

Prepare the cookies to look like the different moon phases:

- One full moon cookie (Take off the top cookie of the Oreo to reveal a white circle of creamy center.)

- One new moon cookie (Use a whole cookie or take off the top cookie and scrape off—and eat!—the white center filling.)

- Two half moon cookies, one waxing and one waning (Remove the top cookie. Scrape off half of the cream.)

- Two crescent moon cookies, one waxing and one waning (Use the knife to etch the shape before removing the cream filling.)

- Two gibbous moon cookies, one waxing and one waning (Remove only a crescent of cream filling.)

- Draw Earth in the middle of the paper.

> ## MATERIALS
> - paper
> - eight Oreo sandwich cookies
> - butter knife
> - colored pens

Cookie Phases

INSTRUCTIONS (continued)

Challenge

Place the eight moon cookies in a circle around Earth to show which moon phases you see from Earth during the lunar cycle.

Label each of the phases WAXING or WANING by noting which side of the moon is lit up. If you are in the northern hemisphere (North America, Europe, or Asia), the moon "grows," or waxes, right to left.

Remember this phrase: "Moon on the right, getting bigger every night."

If you are in the southern hemisphere (Australia, South Africa, or South America), the moon waxes left to right.

After you place all the moon phases around Earth and label them, draw arrows to show the direction of the moon's orbit. Remember, the moon waxes toward the full moon and wanes toward the new moon.

Share your lunar cookie diagram with friends and family. Finally, invite them to eat the different phases of the moon with you!

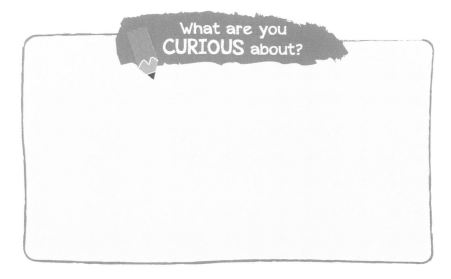

Be a Selenologist!

INSTRUCTIONS

Become familiar with the monthly lunar cycle by direct observation. Keep a Field Journal day to day, week to week, and month to month to get to know our lunar neighbor. Keeping a Field Journal will help you discover these patterns:

- When does the moon rise?

- When does the moon set?

- How long does it take to go from full moon to new moon and back to full moon again?

- How much earlier or later does the moon rise each night or day?

Draw shapes of the dark maria and the round craters. Can you see a shape that looks like the moon bunny or the old man on the moon?

Use the "moon calculator" at timeanddate.com for reference. Choose the Sun&Moon tab. Don't forget to set your location for accurate moonrise and set times (they change each day.) If you don't see the moon at night, be sure to look for it during the day!

Print out as many Field Journal pages (page 25) as you like!

SPECIAL FEATURES
After you've been observing the moon for a while, see if you notice these patterns:

- Which moon phase rises in the east at the end of the day?

- What phase of the moon rises at early dawn?

ACTIVITY
4

Moon Phase Bingo

INSTRUCTIONS

Time to show your deep knowledge of the moon cycle in a game of Moon Phase Bingo!

Preparation

1. Cut out the orbit chips (page 27) and put them in the hat or pouch.

2. Cut out the Moon Phase bingo cards. There are two sets—one for the Northern Hemisphere (pages 29-31) and one for the Southern Hemisphere (pages 33-35).

3. Use chalk to draw a circle as big across as your arm span (about 3–5 feet).

4. Draw Earth in the middle of the circle.

5. Following the sample diagram:

   • Draw the rays of the sun shining from one direction.

   • Write number 1 on the circle closest to the sun.

   • Continue to write the numbers up to 29 around the circle, similar to the numbers on a clock or sundial. Helpful hint: Write 16 on the opposite side of the circle, and 8 and 23 a quarter of the way around. Then fill in the other numbers.

   IMPORTANT: If you are in the **Northern Hemisphere**, make sure the numbers ascend in a **counterclockwise direction**. If you are in the **Southern Hemisphere**, make sure the numbers ascend in a **clockwise direction**.

Playing the Game

Each player chooses a Moon Phase Bingo card (from either the Northern or Southern Hemisphere set).

The first player picks an orbit chip and reads which day of the lunar cycle is printed on the chip. The player then takes the two-tone ball and stands in the

MATERIALS

• chalk

• concrete for drawing (driveway, sidewalk, or playground)

• scissors

• two-tone ball from Activity 1

• objects to use as bingo card markers (e.g., pennies, pebbles, or poker chips)

• hat or pouch for the orbit chips

Moon Phase Bingo

INSTRUCTIONS (continued)

center of the circle. Holding the ball out at arm's length in the direction of the day in the lunar cycle indicated on the orbit chip, the player names the moon phase at this day in the lunar cycle. *Make sure the light side of the ball is facing the direction of the sun.*

All players with a matching Moon Phase on their bingo card get to cover up that space.

The game continues as each player picks an orbit chip, stands on Earth with the moon at arm's length in the direction of the day in the lunar cycle, names the moon phase, and tries to match it to a space on their Moon Phase card.

The first player to cover all the spaces on their Moon Phase card wins!

Note: The moon phases for the days of the lunar orbit are simplified in this activity. In fact, the lunar cycle is 29½ days—or, to be very precise, 29 days, 12 hours, 44 minutes, and 3 seconds! The full, new, and half moon phases are represented by one day in the lunar cycle in this activity, but the moon may appear full or half lit for several days. This is a great topic to discuss, as you may have different opinions of when the moon looks full, gibbous, half, and crescent!

KEY FOR MOON PHASE BINGO

Northern Hemisphere	Phase		Southern Hemisphere
	Day 1	New moon	
	Days 2–7	Waxing crescent	
	Day 8	Waxing half	
	Days 9–15	Waxing gibbous	
	Day 16	Full moon	
	Days 17–22	Waning gibbous	
	Day 23	Waning half	
	Days 24–29	Waning crescent	

Curiosity Connector

Here are some links to help you follow your curiosity!

- Take tours of lunar landing sites, narrated by Apollo astronauts: https://www.google.com/moon/

- Explore videos, lessons, and games to learn more about the moon: neok12.com/Moon.htm

- Learn more facts and tidbits about our neighbor, the moon: https://moon.nasa.gov/about/in-depth/

- Check out this video, which reinforces concepts about phases of the moon: wonderville.ca/asset/phases-of-the-moon

- Use this interactive moon map to explore the maria and craters on the near side of the moon: scientificpsychic.com/etc/moonmap/moon-map.html

- Learn more about what it would be like to be with Selene on the moon: earthsky.org/space/how-often-can-you-see-sunrises-and-sunsets-from-the-moon and https://www.youtube.com/watch?v=-HgHEO0DUig

Cool Moon Ideas to Think About

- One day on the moon lasts a whole lunar month (around 29½ days) since the rotation and revolution periods of the moon are the same. One spin takes as long as one trip around Earth!

- Earth experiences phases, too! Standing on the moon (like Selene in the story), you would see Earth phases during a lunar month. Imagine this … the Earth and moon phases are opposite each other. When you see a FULL moon from Earth, it is a NEW Earth phase from the moon. The day in the lunar cycle when there is a waxing crescent moon from Earth, there is a waning gibbous Earth from the moon!

- **SPECIAL CHALLENGE:** Do Activity 1 again from the perspective of someone standing on the moon. What phases of Earth do you see from the moon as you orbit around Earth?

Glossary

CRATER – a round, bowl-shaped basin on the surface of the moon

CRESCENT – the moon phase when a curved sliver of light is visible

CYCLE – a regular series of events that repeats

FAR – the side of the moon that always faces away from Earth

FULL – the moon phase when the sun and moon are on opposite sides of Earth

GIBBOUS – the moon phase between half and full, when much of the near side is visible

GRAVITY – the natural force that keeps us on the ground and the moon in orbit

LINE OF SIGHT – the view of an object (such as the moon) from a distant point (such as Earth)

LUNAR – having to do with the moon

MARIA (singular MARE) – dark areas of the moon that are made up of heavy volcanic rock

NEAR – the side of the moon that always faces Earth

NEW – the moon phase when the moon is between the sun and Earth

ORBIT – a circular movement, such as the revolution of the moon around Earth

PHASE – any of the possible ways in which the moon appears as viewed from Earth as it orbits Earth during the lunar cycle

REVOLVE – the motion of the moon around Earth (and Earth around the sun)

ROTATES – spins on its axis (such as Earth or the moon)

SELENOLOGIST – a person who studies selenology, the branch of astronomy that deals with the moon

TERRAE – light-colored highlands on the moon that are marked by craters

WANING – describes moon phases as they get smaller toward a new moon

WAXING – describes moon phases as they get bigger toward a full moon

Tools for Your Tool Kit

Let's make the ideas you learned today part of your life tool kit. Remember to print out some blank tool kit pages and tape or glue on today's tools.

1. Starting with the New Moon, list the following moon phases in the order you would see them from Earth:

   WAXING GIBBOUS   FULL MOON   WANING CRESCENT   NEW MOON

   WANING GIBBOUS   WANING HALF   WAXING CRESCENT   WAXING HALF

   _____

   _____

   Add **MOON PHASES** to your tool kit.

2. The moon phases repeat themselves over the course of a lunar month. A pattern that

   repeats itself is called a _____ .   Add **CYCLE** to your tool kit.

3. From Earth, we see light and dark patterns on the moon's surface. These are called the

   _____ and _____ .

   Add **MARIA** and **TERRAE** to your tool kit.

4. It takes the moon 29½ days to travel around Earth. This is called a *revolution* or the lunar

   _____ .   Add **ORBIT** to your tool kit.

Field Journal

ACTIVITY
3

Cutouts for Activity 3: Be a Selenologist!

Date	Time	Drawing of the Moon Phase	Waxing or Waning	Direction in Sky (rising in East, setting in West, overhead)	Observations (craters, orientation, etc.)

Orbit Chips

Day 1	Day 2	Day 3	Day 4
Day 5	Day 6	Day 7	Day 8
Day 9	Day 10	Day 11	Day 12
Day 13	Day 14	Day 15	Day 16
Day 17	Day 18	Day 19	Day 20
Day 21	Day 22	Day 23	Day 24
Day 25	Day 26	Day 27	Day 28

Northern Hemisphere Bingo Cards

Moon Phase Bingo Card (Northern Hemisphere)

Full moon	Waxing crescent	Waxing half	Waxing gibbous

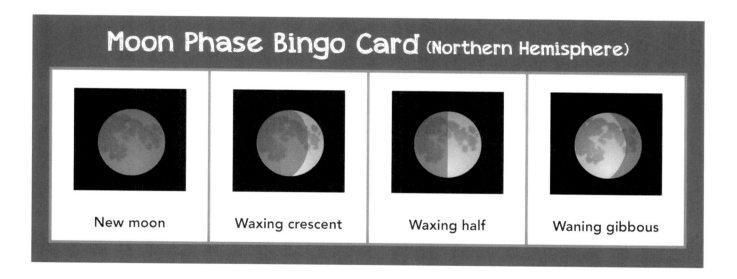

Moon Phase Bingo Card (Northern Hemisphere)

New moon	Waxing crescent	Waxing half	Waning gibbous

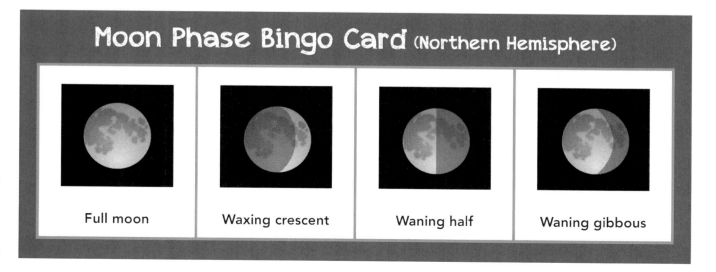

Moon Phase Bingo Card (Northern Hemisphere)

Full moon	Waxing crescent	Waning half	Waning gibbous

Northern Hemisphere Bingo Cards

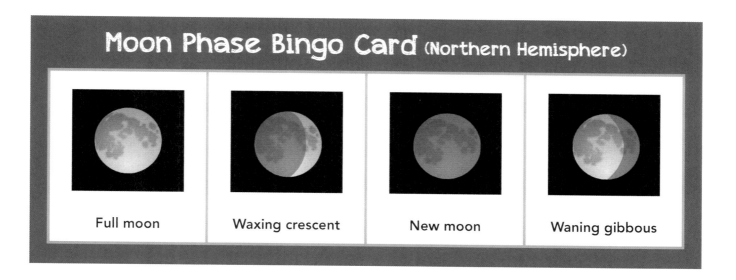

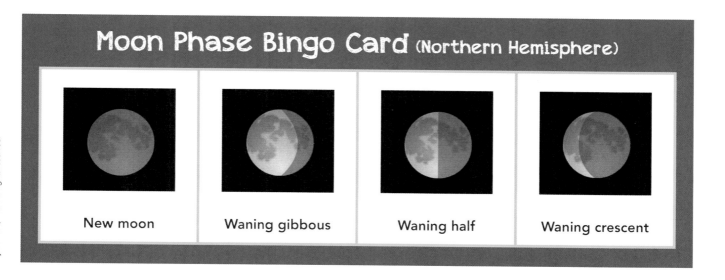

Southern Hemisphere Bingo Cards

Moon Phase Bingo Card (Southern Hemisphere)

Full moon

Waxing crescent

Waxing half

Waxing gibbous

Moon Phase Bingo Card (Southern Hemisphere)

New moon

Waxing crescent

Waxing half

Waning gibbous

Moon Phase Bingo Card (Southern Hemisphere)

Full moon

Waxing crescent

Waning half

Waning gibbous

Southern Hemisphere Bingo Cards

Moon Phase Bingo Card (Southern Hemisphere)

New moon	Waxing crescent	Waning half	Waxing gibbous

Moon Phase Bingo Card (Southern Hemisphere)

Full moon	Waxing crescent	New moon	Waning gibbous

Moon Phase Bingo Card (Southern Hemisphere)

New moon	Waning gibbous	Waning half	Waning crescent

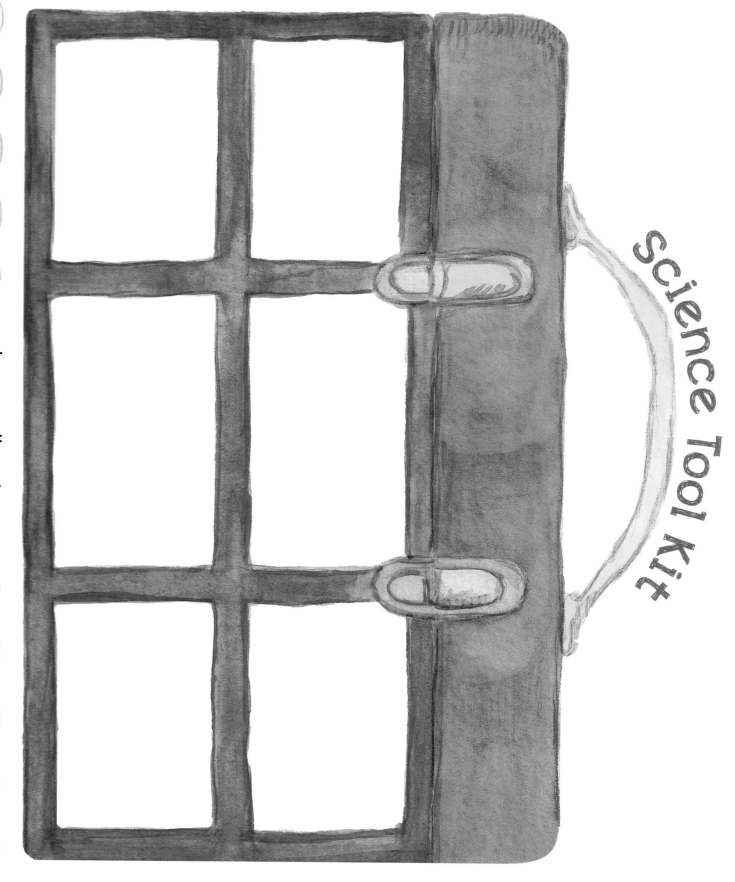

www.benaturallycurious.com

Science Tool Kit

Made in the USA
San Bernardino, CA
29 July 2020